HOW IMPORTANT PEOPLE ACT

Behaving Yourself In Public

bright sky press
HOUSTON, TEXAS

2365 Rice Blvd., Suite 202
Houston, Texas 77005

ISBN: 978-1-939055-96-5

10   9   8   7   6   5   4   3   2

Library of Congress Cataloging-in-Publication Data on file with publisher.
Library of Congress Control Number: 2015933558

Editorial Direction, Lucy Herring Chambers
Editor, Eva J. Freeburn
Design, Marla Y. Garcia

Printed in Korea through Four Colour Print Group

HOW IMPORTANT PEOPLE ACT

Behaving Yourself In Public

CHASE UNTERMEYER

bright sky press

HOUSTON, TEXAS

TABLE OF CONTENTS

ANYONE CAN BECOME IMPORTANT

Are you an Important Person?

You may not be a VIP like a United States senator or a governor or a CEO, and you may not even be a school board member or run your own small business.

But anyone can become an Important Person, sometimes suddenly, depending on circumstances. And when this happens, you need to know that different behavior is expected from you than from everyone else.

As an Important Person, you don't just have a job to do; you also have a role to perform. It is a role that requires you to be *composed, comfortable, confident, and considerate*. It is not a role in which to be snooty or tyrannical. *How Important People Act* tells you how to play this role to perfection, even if it is brand-new to you.

You may already be an Important Person, at least in someone's eyes. It all depends on context. For example:

- You may not be very important in your company, but one day you may receive a promotion to district manager—in charge of a group of states, a part of a state, or just a major neighborhood in a big city. Especially if you live or work in a small community, you automatically become important, because to the people with whom you deal, *you are* the company.
- You may be in charge of charitable giving at your company. It could be just a small part of your daily job, but when you visit a struggling non-profit organization that very much needs the dollars you have to donate, you become all-important to them and what they're trying to do in the community.
- Likewise, your boss may ask you one morning to represent the company on a community board or attend an event where the firm will receive an award. Just like that district manager, all of a sudden you take on the importance of the whole company.
- Your boss may put you in charge of a group of people working on a special project. It may not be anything bigger than the annual picnic, but it will be no less a test of your leadership than being made the chief negotiator on a big merger.
- You may be the president of the parent-teacher organization in your child's school. If the principal needs your help on something, you become very important indeed to her and quite possibly to the education of all the children there.
- You may wear a uniform of some sort—as a police officer, a nurse, or a military recruiter. You may be a very tiny part of the big organization to which you belong, but to the

citizens who see you at any given moment, you take on the importance of the entire city, hospital, or armed force, whose very visible emblem you are right then.

- The clergy likewise are Important People, because they stand for something greater than mortal flesh: God (in all names), the Church, Jesus, the Prophet Mohammed, Buddha, etc. The humblest parish priest, calling on the home of the poorest believer, is a person of unimaginable importance. And there is special importance in being the *spouse* of a member of the clergy, particularly in a small community.
- You may be sent abroad on a business trip, where you may suddenly find yourself in a leadership role, simply because you represent a company that matters to the people you're meeting. In many countries, you may discover you're important in local eyes simply because of your nationality. This puts an extra burden upon you, for you will not only embody your company but your country as well. The impression you make on the people you meet may determine forever how they think about both.
- Or you could be *really* important: The high school football coach in a West Texas town!

There's an old saying: "Some are born great; some achieve greatness; and some have greatness thrust upon them." The same is true with leadership. Some leaders are born—royalty, for example, or members of famous wealthy families. Others strive for years to make themselves leaders by determinedly climbing the corporate ladder to ever-higher positions; by seeking and winning public office at all levels; by rising in the ranks of the military, law enforcement, or the church; by becoming a sports or entertainment star; and so forth. And then there are the vast number of people who suddenly have leadership thrust upon them in the many everyday ways suggested earlier.

When the time comes that you are an Important Person, you need to be aware of the one abiding fact of life for everyone in this category: *People will be watching you.* Partly this is because human beings are curious about celebrities, even very junior-grade ones. It may also be because they've got nothing better to do, and you're the one who is sitting or standing in front of them on a platform. Those with an evil turn of mind may be watching purely in the hope of seeing you mess up.

President Barack Obama and First Lady Michelle Obama attended the memorial service for one of history's truly great men, Nelson Mandela, in South Africa in December 2013. There were long delays in the service, and to break the boredom the President and the prime ministers of Great Britain and Denmark made a "selfie" of themselves smiling broadly.

Put aside the fact this was inappropriately light-hearted behavior at such a solemn event. The amazing thing is that the three leaders—all experienced and savvy politicians, used to having cameras trained on them all the time—somehow forgot that literally the whole world was watching. Photos of the "selfie" shot around the world within moments of its occurrence, bringing harsh and justified criticism of the participants for engaging in such an antic at such a time. (The First Lady, sitting apart from the merry group, acted with great dignity and respect.)

What all this means, for leaders of nations and PTOs alike, is that you have to be extra careful of what you do and say. You don't have to freeze with fear over this prospect. Important People at all levels of life can be relaxed, good-natured, and effective in what they do, simply by applying the secrets, hints, and tricks listed in this little book.

How Important People Act is not an etiquette book that tells you which fork to use. It is not a book on protocol that tells you how to address an archbishop. It is not a how-to-succeed book that helps you make the next big sale. Nor is it a guide to acting high-toned. You don't have to act any way other than your natural self. What this book teaches are ways of dealing easily and comfortably with such ordinary functions as going to a banquet, attending a funeral, taking a tour, meeting people in a reception, and wearing a nametag—plus some special circumstances in which you may find yourself, like giving a speech, running a meeting, or traveling overseas on business.

This book can also be of value to shy people who feel awkward in social settings. The techniques described can actually give you an edge over the more dazzling types who, because of the blessing of their looks, have felt since babyhood that they don't have to try very hard to be loved. They imagine that the entire world adores them, much as they do themselves. We've all known such people, those who are so smitten with themselves that they become lazy, arrogant, and vain—in short, most *un*attractive. The shy person who knows ways of making others feel comfortable and appreciated can win over those whom the dazzlers turn off.

This is the embodiment of the Golden Rule: Treating others as you would have them treat you. It is the perfect blending of good values, good manners, and devastatingly effective behavior.

Finally, throughout the book you will find boxes like this one. Inside are **Tips for Very Important People *(Tips for VIPs)*.** While you may never need this particular advice, you're allowed to peek—and see how these people effortlessly carry off the challenge of always being in the public eye.

So, here is how Important People act and how ordinary people who assume leadership can, with all eyes watching them, pull it off like a pro.

So let's start with the basics: The clothes on your back.

Veep Freeze: What not to wear at the next somber occasion.

Chapter 1

LOOKING GOOD

The first essential is to look good. You may not be Hollywood's idea of good-looking, but that doesn't matter. The goal is to be the best-looking *you* possible.

In these self-consciously casual times, when the official uniform of prince and president alike seems to be the open-necked shirt, the old rules of dress seem to have been thrown out with the club tie. This is because it is deemed stuffy or "elitist" nowadays for an Important Person, even a VIP, to dress any differently from ordinary folk. It is a sort of sartorial democracy, enforced by image-makers in places like London, New York, Washington, Toronto, and LA.

But this totally misreads the way things are. People expect and want Important People to be different from them. They imagine leaders to be brighter, more dynamic, and more successful than they are. And they think this, not out of self-abasement, but because we always need people who set the standard, who can be looked up to—in short, who are leaders. This is true at all levels of society and in all places.

The best proof of this came during the Great Depression, when millions of Americans were out of work, had little to eat, and had only a few well-worn clothes to wear. The man whom they again and again elected president of the United States did not dress like them or talk like them but wore silk hats and striped trousers and spoke with a Harvard accent. He was of course Franklin Delano Roosevelt.

It wasn't FDR's clothes that gave him the ability to radiate confidence during the Depression. It was the sum of everything he was and everything he had done in his life. Roosevelt felt no need to apologize or humble himself because of his gilded origins, and so he dressed the way he always had. Not even the poorest American resented him for doing so. In fact, they *expected* the President to dress as he did.

Equally unapologetic about clothing was his wife, Eleanor, who came from the same lofty background as her husband. Though critics snidely called her "dowdy," Eleanor dressed as was natural to a woman of her upbringing. When, legend says, someone asked Mrs. Roosevelt where she bought her clothes, she replied, "One does not buy clothes; one *has* clothes." It was this unaffected comfort with who she was, reflected in what she wore, that made the thousands of impoverished people she met during the 1930s feel at ease with the First Lady of the Land.

At the other end of the fashion scale from Eleanor Roosevelt was Jacqueline Bouvier Kennedy, who also conveyed a strong and positive message by what she wore. When her husband John F. Kennedy was running in the crucial West Virginia presidential primary in 1960, some of his advisors worried that voters in that very poor state would recoil against Jacqueline if she made public appearances dressed as she normally did, which was elegantly. But she wore in Wheeling what she wore in Washington, and instead of turning off the voters she beguiled them—and helped JFK win the primary.

In the riotous 1960s, when traditional ways of doing things were being upended daily, the great popular figures were President Kennedy and Martin Luther King Jr., two men who never thought of appearing in public without a firmly-knotted necktie. People tittered when a photograph was published showing President Richard Nixon walking on the beach in lace-up shoes. But it would have looked even more ridiculous for the President of the US to be in flip-flops.

President Jimmy Carter began the modern bent of presidents to dress casually, wearing sweaters and shirts demurely open at the collar. This may have been a studied reaction to "the imperial presidency" of his recent predecessor, Nixon, from whom neckties had to be surgically removed. Carter's time in the White House, the late 1970s, was when men and women looked their silliest in all American history. So, compared with fellow males who sported long hair, flamboyant sideburns and mustaches, flared trousers, and shirts open to the navel, Carter was a model of leader-like dignity.

If re-election was Carter's political dress-for-success goal, he failed. The regular folks, who he so much wanted to like him, turned instead (in the election of 1980) to Ronald Reagan, who represented older virtues and manners. In contrast to the casual Carter, Reagan never removed his jacket in the Oval Office, out of respect for what the room signified and the role he had been chosen to fill.

The times may have also played a role in how citizens literally saw their presidents: Carter's sweaters may have seemed fine when the world was relatively calm. But let Iranian students seize American diplomats and Russians run rampant in Afghanistan, and people wanted someone who looked (and was) in command. Put another way, they didn't want a president who would unbutton his collar so much as one who would button up the ayatollahs and the Kremlin. This is what Reagan, with a sense of style and its subconscious power acquired in Hollywood's golden days, instinctively gave America.

Reagan also shrewdly knew when to wear *less* clothing, as when he was photographed in a T-shirt chopping brush on his ranch or appearing outdoors in Iceland with Mikhail Gorbachev in just a business suit while his Soviet counterpart was bundled in a hat and heavy overcoat. Both images projected Reagan as healthy and strong, important for a public man in his eighth decade of life.

Unfortunately, Reagan's successors seemed to believe that democracy demands that its leaders dress the same as their constituents, and denizens of both the Screen Actors Guild and the White House sank into studied casualness and sometimes outright sloppiness.

Vice President Dick Cheney represented the United States at a somber event in Poland in 2005 commemorating the liberation of the infamous Auschwitz concentration camp sixty years before. It was a cold January day, and Presidents Jacques Chirac of France and Vladimir Putin of Russia wore dark overcoats and dress shoes, befitting both the weather and the ceremony. By contrast, the Veep wore a furry parka, snow boots, and a knit ski cap—which *The Washington Post* sniffed was what "one typically wears to operate a snow blower.[1]" Cheney is a down-to-earth guy from Wyoming, and his choice of clothing that day bespoke his very practical nature. But it did not reflect the importance placed by the United States on the occasion.

- For men in business settings, the right "uniform" is a dark suit, a white shirt, a necktie, and polished shoes. Increasingly, it is acceptable to wear the suit without a tie, but the necktie (uncomfortable though it may be) is a sign of maturity and seriousness. After all, you're not dressing to impress people but to win their confidence. This is why radio announcers of the BBC (British Broadcasting Corporation) used to wear tuxedoes and black tie when they read the news. No one could see them, but the formal dress reinforced their professionalism and added to the authority in their voices.

Women likewise convey competence and authority by wearing dresses and suits with modest jewelry.

---

[1] Reuters, quoted by CNN.com, "Cheney's Auschwitz outfit raises eyebrows", 28 January 2005.

- So, the rule is: ***Dress up, not down.*** This doesn't mean wearing black tie or evening dress to a picnic. But whatever level of dress the occasion calls for, you should look your best. The casual look may work in Silicon Valley, but start-ups should dress up when they go to the offices of investment bankers. And when casual clothes are appropriate, they should be attractive, tidy, and modest rather than grungy or revealing.
- In fact, a good rule for the Important Person is to ***show less skin rather than more***. That means long sleeves (which can always be rolled up) rather than short sleeves; buttons buttoned rather than left undone; and trousers rather than shorts.

Only on very rare occasions might it be better to go bare. President Theodore Roosevelt liked to lead members of his Cabinet, ranking military officers, and foreign diplomats on vigorous romps in the wilder reaches around Washington. One hot day, hiking with such a group near Chain Bridge in Virginia, TR proposed a cooling swim in the Potomac. They stripped down to nothing—all except French ambassador Jules Jusserand, whose black kid gloves remained on his manicured hands. When the President remarked on this amusing oddity, Jusserand explained, "We might meet ladies."[2]

- Young men today often go without shaving for more than just the weekend. They may think this makes them look hip or tough, and perhaps to their peers it does. But to anyone who may be considering them for a job or a promotion, it makes them look sloppy and careless. So,

---

[2] Edmund Morris. *Theodore Rex*. New York: Random House, 2001.

guys, unless you're auditioning for a beer commercial, use the razor on weekday mornings.

- If you're not sure what to wear to an event—and invitations these days can be unhelpful, listing the dress as "tropical chic" or "black tie optional"— observe the rule followed by U.S. Marines: **When in doubt, dress up**. Whether in dress blues for a parade or in camouflage for combat, the Marines always look great, reinforcing their image as leaders. Your daily mission may only require you to storm the Halls of Manhattan and the Shores of Santa Monica, but you can take a lesson from the men and women in green.
- Women consider shoes a vital part of their ensemble and want admiring eyes drawn to their feet as much as to other parts of their person. This is not the case with men, who should avoid wearing shoes or socks that call attention to themselves.
- Whatever is worn nowadays below the neck, the one place democracy rules (without a quibble from this book) is on top of the head. The ball cap has become not just the American hat of choice but also the world's. It's simple, fun, practical, cheap, and comes in so many varieties that by simple change of cap the Important Person can be right in line with the group he or she is visiting. Just be sure to wear the visor in the front.

Dressing your best doesn't make you a snob, nor should it give you a sense of superiority over others. On the contrary, as demonstrated by Jimmy Carter on one end and the Marine Corps on the other, the better you look the better people will think of you, regardless of what they themselves are wearing.

*A trifecta of errors: Glass in right hand, nametag on left,
and not looking at who's talking.*

- Chapter 2 -

MAKING AN APPEARANCE & NOT A SPECTACLE

An Important Person's reason to attend a reception or banquet may be simply to show support for an organization or a cause. A VIP (like a politician) may do the same but also wants to meet as many people as possible before moving on to another function. Whichever circumstance you find yourself in, here is what you need to know.

- *"Hello, I'm the Speaker."* As soon as you arrive, **seek out the person in charge to reassure them that you're there.** If you've had trouble parking, finding the venue, or you were simply using the restroom, they may have gone into panic and sent people out looking for you. Establish what you'll need to know: When things will really start, when you'll have to speak or present something, and where they want you to sit.
- *The Nametag:* More mistakes are made with this common appliance than you may realize. The people producing the tags may write or print the names too small to read, which, after all, is the purpose of the nametag. Or, if the name is legible in normal light, it can't be made out in the low lighting that some people think makes a cocktail party

glamorous. Whether or not such a dim-watted idea lends glamour to an occasion, it certainly lends mystery—as in, "Who am I talking to?"

There is only one proper place for a nametag, as decreed in the *First Law of Nametags:*

Always wear it on the right!
When we meet someone we unconsciously look at the right-hand side; after all, that's where the hand we're shaking is located. Since most people are right-handed, they naturally slap the nametag onto their left side or (if they're the eager helper at the registration table) place it on the left side of the person standing in front of them.

When it comes to reading the nametag of the person you're meeting, try to do this before you shake hands. This will let you maintain eye contact with the person while shaking his hand—even if at that moment his eyes are darting down to read *your* nametag.

Don't make the common mistake of leaving your nametag on when you get up and speak. This is because that rectangle of white on your dress or lapel is a subconscious distraction to the eye, especially if it's encased in shiny plastic or hung with ribbons reading "Speaker" or "Director." When you speak, you want all eyes on your face, not on your shoulder.

Therefore, the *Second Law of Nametags:*

Take it off before speaking!
You can always put it on again during the prolonged standing ovation that will surely follow your remarks.

Finally, there is the *Third Law of Nametags:*

Take it off before being photographed!
This will prevent a picture in which you look as if you have a label.

- *"Your name is familiar, but I forget your face."* Small books on sale at supermarket checkout counters boast 1001 handy ways to remember names, and maybe they can. This book makes no such claim. But perhaps it can render another sort of service with names.

The best thing, of course, is to remember everyone's name. But the worst thing is not forgetting a name; it's *pretending* you remember it when you very clearly don't. Somewhere in between lies a good general rule for life: *If you can't remember a person's name, simply say, "I'm sorry, I don't recall your name."*

This unusual burst of honesty, especially from an Important Person, can impress people almost as much as actually remembering their name. It can in fact be positively disarming, for it shows you care enough to *want* to know who they are. And this gesture may be more valuable to you than never forgetting a name.

Every Important Person has to endure the jerk who says, "I bet you don't remember me." One's first impulse is to smile sweetly and respond, "Yer darn right I don't, and I don't give a flip, neither!" But this should be resisted in favor of a more earnest answer: *"Sorry, I don't remember. Give me a clue."* Once again, such a response will show the other fellow that you want to know his name, even when he so clearly deserves to be forgotten.

- *The Most Important Thing of All:* No one expects the kind of gab conducted during a stand-up function to be deep, fulfilling, or even audible. But there is one absolute thing to do with everyone with whom you talk: *You want the person to feel that, for you, during those few moments, he or she is the only person on earth.*

Precisely nobody is deceived by the hearty glad hander who barks "Great to see you!" while looking over your shoulder for someone greater to see. And yet it happens again and again, to the point that the benefit of the handshake is lost. That is why the unexpected and very personal encounter can be so smashingly successful.

The real masters of this art form—and Presidents Bill Clinton, George W. Bush, and Barack Obama are grand masters—can focus their attention on the person with them in such an intense way that, both to them and the object of this treatment, everyone and everything else around them is blotted out.

It is said that "timing is everything in politics." This time is usually reckoned in years (*Do I try for the Senate next year or the time after that?*), months (*When do I announce my candidacy?*), days (*When do we run that TV spot?*), hours (*When should that press release be issued?*), or minutes (*When do I spring my practiced put-down during this debate?*) But truly successful politicians know that the most crucial timing is measured in *seconds*: namely, the few moments that he or she is shaking hands with someone and enveloping that voter in the silken web of deep personal interest.

The test of this skill—and, from the other person's viewpoint, the proof that you really do care about him or her—comes when someone else tries to break in. The extra split-seconds that you maintain eye contact are almost a way of saying, "What nerve this creep has to interrupt when I really want to talk to *you*! But—*sigh*—I suppose I have to pay attention to him. Sorry; perhaps another time...."

George W. Bush's technique for dealing with such interlopers is to drape his arm over the newcomer's shoulder while continuing to talk to the first person. It signals that the newcomer is next in line to get the full you're-the-only-person-on-earth treatment.

MAKING MAXIMUM CONTACT

VIPs need to keep conversations short enough so that they can continue moving through the crowd and meeting more people. You may have an aide, a young man or woman who will remorselessly extract you from the clutches of someone on whom your intense gaze has worked perhaps a little too well. Lacking an aide, you can ask the hosts of a function to have someone help you meet attendees. Then *he* will get the dirty and disappointed looks, not you.

If you need to escape an overlong conversation and move on, you can hand the person a business card and say, "I'd really like to continue our talk. Why don't you give me a call next week?" Or you can ask politely, "May I get you something from the bar?" and hope the person says no. Of course, with some babblers nothing works better than a polite but firm insertion of "I've very much enjoyed talking with you!" as you shake hands and dash away.

After all, the risk of meeting new bores is worth spending additional awful minutes with the one who's already found you.

Tips for VIPs # 2:
THE IRISH REEL

There is a technique perfected by those ultimate schmoozers, Boston Irish politicians. It involves speaking with one person while shaking hands with a second and smiling at a third. But only a few gifted pols—such as its all-time champion practitioner, Mayor John F. (Honey Fitz) Fitzgerald, grandfather of President Kennedy—can get away with it. It is the conversational equivalent of standing on your head while riding a bicycle.

- *Have You Met Miss Jones?* Etiquette books lay down a procedure for introducing people that is often befuddling in practice. It decrees that you introduce the junior person in age and rank to the senior person and introduce men to women. This requires speaking the senior person's or the woman's name first. This can quickly become a tangled mess: What if the junior person is a woman? Who is older here? Who outranks whom? Quick, get the etiquette book!

But none of this really matters, except in the most formal of circumstances, which are fairly rare ("Your Eminence, may I present Chuckles the Clown?"). The rule is simply introduce people. In real life, the true breach of good manners comes in not making sure that all the people standing around you know each other. True, the Important Person may be the center of attention, but he or she should always strive to make others feel at ease. That means including everyone in the conversation, so that they're talking with each other as much as with you.

There's a practical benefit to the Important Person who succeeds at this gambit: If the conversation really gets going, you can slip away more easily to be with other people without seeming abrupt or rude.

Following this simple rule means that sometimes you will introduce people who have known each other since childhood. When this happens, a few lame humorists will say, "Oh, I've never seen her before in my life!" This has the unfortunate effect of scaring many a well-meaning introducer out of ever trying that again. But two shy people standing nearby, appearing to listen to you but silently yearning to know each other, may never meet otherwise. You could be responsible for a great romance!

Finally, always introduce yourself. This is of course necessary with people you've never met and with those you've met before but whose name is a momentary blank. Even if you are a person whom everyone knows, there may be someone (especially after a couple of drinks) who doesn't recognize you or who imagines you to be younger/older/shorter/taller than you actually are. Also, the Important Person who introduces himself or herself displays a certain attractive humility. It shows you don't think you're so important that everyone ought to know who you are.

Tips for VIPs #3
NEXT IN LINE!

Many a society hostess claims she has proved that no one pays attention to anything said in a receiving line. As guests filed past, she would brightly say, "Good evening! I just shot my husband!" Whereupon each person would beam, murmur something like, "How nice!" and move on.

Whether or not anyone ever actually tried this and got away with it, receiving lines are wearisome relics. But, should you find yourself in one, the fact you may have to meet scores, even hundreds, of complete strangers does not relieve you of trying to make each person feel special.

Remembering each person's name is not as important as repeating it, all the while looking them directly in the eye for an unbroken number of seconds while warmly shaking (or, in the case of women, squeezing) their hand.

If you are hosting a VIP in a receiving line, you should give him or her little clues about each person: "Senator, you remember Gladys Gulch, who addressed envelopes for you in Ward 6 during the last campaign?" The VIP can easily take things from there: "Why, of course! Gladys, how are you? Thanks for your help with all those envelopes!"

A final thing to remember is to *keep the line moving,* so someone who really does want to tell you how they're doing can be politely moved along. This will allow others to meet the VIP and (probably more importantly) proceed to the bar.

• *Nibbling:* A particular challenge at stand-up functions is eating. Unless you're starving, don't eat at receptions. The hazards are too great and too awful to contemplate: Talking with your mouth full; dropping something on yourself; spewing it on the person with whom you're speaking; morsels of food left lurking between the teeth; and bad breath from something garlicky or fishy.

If hunger is causing you to grow faint, go for the things that are drier, whiter, and odorless, like the pieces of French bread arrayed for the cheese—but not the cheese itself.

And watch out for the crumbs!

- *Eating Large:* Big public luncheons or dinners carry special risks for an Important Person, because that's when you are most on view.

There are still many functions with a traditional head table on a raised platform called the dais (pronounced "day-us" or "die-us'). At other events, the head table looks the same as all other tables, only it's placed near the platform or stage. In this more intimate setting, you may be hard to spot until the moment you are introduced to speak.

No matter how many people may be to your right and left, behind you or in front of you, a banquet is a place where truly all eyes can be upon you. So, here are some things to keep in mind:

- *Chow Down before Going Downtown:* A wise rule is: Eat before you go to a banquet. This will keep you from the horrors of the meal and let you avoid a rumbly, grumbly stomach if the event starts late. You may have to sit through endless opening speeches, a fashion show, awards, announcements, and a children's dance performance before they serve the salad.

- *There are few attractive ways to eat when hundreds of people may be watching you. Our mothers told us not to talk with our mouths full, but how else can you talk during a meal?* The answer is: Appear to be eating. Not having to deal with the meal means you can enjoy talking with the person next to you and risk being photographed at the same time. Simply slice the slab of gray meat on your plate once or twice, rearrange it thoughtfully, and spear a mini zucchini with your fork now and then.

Tips for VIPs # 4
THE ULTIMATE SACRIFICE FOR YOUR COUNTRY

It is said that Presidents Nixon and Ford always ate cottage cheese with catsup at political fundraisers. Before you gag, consider the wisdom of their choice of cuisine: From long experience on what politicians call "the rubber chicken circuit," the two presidents knew they had to be seen eating something. They could shovel down great quantities of this bland, tummy-friendly mixture and look like they were eating the same thing as everyone else.

- *Protecting Your Waistline:* There is dietary danger from a regular intake of banquet food, especially the high-priced fare that comes drizzled with a fine reduction of something fattening.

The best preventative here is something else your mother used to tell you. Remember when you were a kid and your family would go out to eat? You'd grab the basket of bread or crackers and start gobbling them down, whereupon Mom would say, "Don't eat that! It'll spoil your appetite."

Precisely, Mom: At luncheons and dinners, spoil your appetite by filling up on the bread so that you're not the least bit tempted to eat much of the main course. Bread may be off your diet, but probably so is most of what's served at the typical banquet: Cream gravies, potatoes au gratin, and of course gooey desserts. If you have any appetite left after downing a roll or two, then follow another of Mom's rules and eat your veggies first.

- *Drinking:* Needless to say, getting drunk at public events does not improve your standing in business, politics, society—or with the police on the drive home. Fortunately, we live in a time when it is entirely acceptable to ask for water or a soft drink instead of a cocktail or to take a glass of weak white wine. It is even permissible not to drink anything at all. This often happens anyway to the Important Person who is so mobbed by friends and admirers that he can't get a drink of any sort.

The key thing to remember, regardless what you're drinking, is always hold the glass in your left hand! This is another thing that most right-handed people forget. After all, when meeting people you don't want to keep shifting the glass to your left hand and extending a cold, wet hand for someone to shake. Ugh!

The Elbow-in-the-Soup Treatment (It worked for Auntie Corinne.)

Chapter 3

CONVERSE—OR WORSE

Whether at a stand-up reception or a sit-down dinner, one of the hardest things to do is talk with total strangers. If the other person is shy, tongue-tied, or bored, you may have to be the one who kicks things off conversationally.

There are all the usual topics: The other person's job, the weather, travel plans, and the like. But the best technique may be one reportedly used by Queen Elizabeth II.

- *The Queen's Trick:* Royalty are expected to meet thousands of people each year and to talk to a goodly number of them. According to protocol, they talk first, and they typically ask questions. Her Majesty asks, ***"What is your current project?"***

This is a brilliant way to start a conversation. The other person could be a famous writer, the owner of a fishing fleet, a foreign diplomat, or an elderly homemaker, but all have something they're currently doing and are probably eager to talk about, even if it's just repainting the kitchen. This allows the Queen to ask a further question or merely give her famous response to something she hears: "Oh, really?" By then, it's time to move on. The people the Queen meets are left feeling that she was genuinely interested in them.

It's usually fairly crass to ask another person, "What do you do?" So, with both sexes, a safe and useful opening question is, "What keeps you busy during the week?" It's different, refreshing, and open-ended enough to allow the other person to mention a job, a hobby, or a tale of family life—any of which can spark further conversation.

- **Can't take my eyes off of you:** If you want to convey the impression that you really care about people, nothing is simpler or more effective than to **look at them when they are talking.** This seems obvious, except that in conversation people are often looking somewhere else—at their food, at their phone, or at others in the room. The fact you're looking straight at someone will make you seem alert, sympathetic, and obviously intelligent—all without saying a word.
- **Let me gaze into the bridge of your nose...** In western culture, it is considered a sign of sincerity and manful directness to look someone straight in the eye. In certain eastern cultures, however, this is considered rude, and polite people tend to avert their eyes from the other person. In any event, it is hard for a shy or nervous person to look straight at someone, particularly if that person is looking at *you* straight in the eye.

The trick is: **Concentrate on the bridge of the other person's nose.** (If he wears eyeglasses, then focus on the nosepiece.) It is a neutral, non-threatening place where you can look at great length and not be spooked by the icy eyes staring back at you. Better yet, the other person can't tell the difference. Try it!

- **But enough about me...** People always would rather talk about themselves (or their families) than anything else. This is especially true if they are nervous or if they are raging egotists, and nervous egotists can talk endlessly. With such people, you may have no recourse but to let them jabber away. This will, after all, allow you to eat your supper, and somewhere along the way you might even hear something interesting. James Reston, the longtime Washington bureau chief of *The New York Times*, harvested many a scoop simply by being an attentive dinner partner at capital soirées. "People love to talk about themselves," he observed. "You get more news by trust than by tricks."[3]

So, the best rule is **always keep the conversation on the other person.** In addition to putting this person at ease, it gives you a chance, while they're gabbing on, to eat, to think about something else, or to overhear a more interesting conversation across the table. The German ambassador to Washington before America entered World War I was said to owe his success in gathering diplomatic intelligence to his "infinite capacity to be bored" at dinner parties.

---

[3] *Reader's Digest,* April 1996, p.50

The sister of President Theodore Roosevelt was a master of this trick. "Auntie Corinne had a great facility for feigning interest," recalled Alice Roosevelt Longworth. "It was known as her 'elbow-in-the-soup treatment.' We were left speechless with admiration at her ability to show interest in some bore's discourse. She would gaze at him intently, hanging on every word. It was a magnificent performance."[4]

Sometimes, when you're eavesdropping on something *really* interesting while a bore drones on, he or she may suddenly stop and (perhaps because they also read this book) ask *you* something. When this happens, quickly say something like, "I'll answer that in a moment. But there was something you said a moment ago that fascinated me—that part about your mother…" This tactic will rev them up again for a good five more minutes!

- *Ask the unexpected:* Celebrities are often asked the same things, over and over, and therefore approach every new conversation primed for boredom. A politician may always be asked about his more popular wife. A CEO may always be asked about a product. A movie star may always be asked about one particular picture or costar. The thing that will spark a real conversation is to **ask them something they don't normally get asked.**

The trick is to ask a variant of the same question: ***"What do you like to do when you're not [doing-what-you're-famous-for]?"*** The senator may be delighted to tell about his golf game, the CEO about his art collection, and the movie star

[4] Michael Teague. *Mrs. L: Conversations with Alice Roosevelt Longworth.*New York: Doubleday, 1981

about his cooking. And chances are, they'll consider you a terrific conversationalist!

- *My compliments!* The same technique applies to praising someone: *Compliment him on something he isn't normally told.*

When John F. Kennedy met Norman Mailer, then most celebrated for his novel *The Naked and the Dead*, he complimented the writer on a lesser-known work, *Deer Park*. Mailer then spread the word how well-read this guy Kennedy was!

Spanish foreign minister José Maria de Areilza met Margaret Thatcher when she was not yet prime minister of Great Britain. He exclaimed: "I had been told, madam, of your formidable intelligence, but no one had warned me of your beauty!"[5]

You might praise a famous musician for his charming interview in that morning's paper. With a governor you might commend a less well-known program of hers you've seen in action. Or if talking to an actor you might say how much you admired his statement to Congress on the need to protect native crab grasses.

Beware making the gaffe, about which every renowned actor has a story, of praising him or her for a play or movie in which he or she did *not* appear.

---

[5] Douglas Hurd . *Memoirs*. Boston: Little, Brown & Co. , 2003

- *The walls (or at least the people at the next table) have ears*: Nothing an Important Person says in a public setting can be considered entirely private, even if it's a confidence to an intimate friend or relative. The person you want to hear your unflattering comment about the hostess or your criticism of the Big Boss may not betray you, but someone nearby may be eavesdropping on you and repeat (or distort) your words without the slightest reluctance. There's also the danger, to which even presidents often fall prey, of the "hot mike," a microphone they think isn't picking up their words but is.

Sometimes Important People forget that things they consider routine and unremarkable might be extremely juicy to others and thus let down their guard. So, *act as if your private words were being broadcast*—because that's exactly what might happen tomorrow morning!

In any event, *speak softly.*

Biden his time while the boss is speaking.

- Chapter 4 -

BEING EXPOSED IN PUBLIC

The Important Person faces risks when seated on a stage or at a head table, even if doing nothing more than listening to someone else speak. If you pay strict attention to the following rules, you can look composed, intelligent, and alert. If you don't, you may look inattentive, rude, or downright goofy.

The most important, most basic rule is: ***Remember, all eyes are upon you!*** Actually, they may not be. They may be focused on the inattentive, rude, or downright goofy person sitting to your right. But you must always act as if everyone is looking at you at all times, because at least one someone will be. (And so will cameras!)

Nancy Reagan was often twitted for the "fixed gaze" she gave her husband when he spoke. The truth is, she was crazy about the guy and hung on his every word.

But imagine what would have happened if, instead of fixing her gaze on Ronnie, Mrs. R had studied the ceiling, chatted with the person next to her, waved to friends in the audience, fidgeted with her clothes or jewelry, and the like. She would have drawn attention to herself, not the speaker, and her inattention would have screamed to the audience that he wasn't worth listening to.

While John F. Kennedy was giving his stirring inaugural address on January 20, 1961, his vice president, Lyndon Johnson, did something quite odd: Sitting in clear view of the cameras, LBJ leaned over to pick up a piece of paper he noticed lying on the platform. He then took out his reading glasses and thoroughly examined both sides of the paper before tucking it into his coat pocket. We never learned what the political master of Washington found so intriguing about that piece of paper, but his action told sixty million viewers that he wasn't much interested in what his new boss had to say.[6]

Then there was Reagan's vice president, George Bush the elder. At joint sessions of Congress, where he sat just behind the President, the VP did not fix his gaze on the boss. Instead, to the exasperation of his staff, he looked all around the chamber; he exchanged jokes with the speaker of the House, and—the absolute worst—he took out his handkerchief and elaborately blew his nose like a character in a silent movie. Bush was an experienced pol who knew a thing or two about TV cameras. Yet on such occasions he somehow thought he was invisible.

Looking inattentive during a State of the Union address may be a vice-presidential thing. Joe Biden, Barack Obama's #2, was seen on TV pointing and grinning at old congressional chums and tapping away on his iPad while the President

---

[6] "Ask Not, Tell Not", *New Yorker*, 8 November 2004.

spoke of serious subjects. The clear unstated message Biden sent millions of viewers was "I've got more fun things to do than listen to *him*."

You don't have to be vice president of the United States to commit the same sort of mistake. You've probably done it quite a lot: A business meeting is dragging on or a speaker is only on page 37 of his PowerPoint presentation…your phone is close at hand…and you take it out to see if a text, tweet, or email has come through in the two minutes since you checked it the last time. Sometimes you do this even when the meeting is important and when you are actually interested in what's being said.

It's just a habit—but a bad one, for it makes the clear and strong statement to everyone that you are more interested in what *might* be on your phone than in what is happening around you. This practice will be seen by others as insulting, unprofessional, juvenile, or simply rude.

So, even when things are truly boring in a business meeting or a public event, resist the temptation to haul out your phone and see what's there. Wait till there's a break. This leads us to a basic rule, similar to the one about good conversation:

- *Since you've got to look somewhere, look at the speaker.* With a little practice, you'll be amazed at how freely and fancifully your mind can wander away from whatever is being said, all the while seeming to pay rapt attention. And whether or not you actually are listening to the speaker, *sit still.*

- *Mine eyes have seen the glory...*Maybe so, but *when a prayer is given, keep your eyes closed.* You may also bow your head and clasp your hands if you wish, but *don't move* until the preacher says, "Amen!" It is remarkable how many Important People stand wide-eyed and inattentive during invocations or benedictions. (Yes, this means your author has peeked!) Whether or not you are a religious person, closing your eyes is a display of simple respect, particularly to believers.

Tips for VIPs # 5
THE WAVE

The writer William F. Buckley once observed that British royalty wave as if reaching up to unscrew a light bulb. A less stiff way to accomplish the same purpose when you're introduced is to stand, extend your arm, and pretend you're giving a final buff to a freshly-polished brass plate somewhere above your head. In other words, the pivot point is not your wrist but your elbow. It certainly isn't your shoulder: There's no need to wag your arm back and forth as if trying to stop a speeding truck.

How to stay awake: When a speaker is droning on; when the dinner was perhaps a bit too ample and the wine too good; or when you may not have gotten a full night's sleep, there comes a time when the drowsies start to overwhelm you, and then...*Plop!* This can be a nightmare for anyone, especially for the Important Person on very public display. But there is a simple remedy.

You've heard the expression "He had me on the edge of my chair!" Well, the speaker who's causing you to drift off into slumber-land may not fit that description, but there is wisdom here: *Sit on the edge of your seat,* leaning slightly forward to provide better balance, and turn your head in the direction of the speaker. This will have the double advantage of not only keeping you perfectly clear-headed but also of making it seem you actually understand (and are fascinated by) what the old bird is saying.

A former ambassador claimed that this technique enabled him to sit through two and a half hours of a very boring address by the president of the country to which he was assigned. It does seem to work. Maybe it's from the adrenalin rush that comes with fear of possibly falling on the floor and really making a spectacle.

- *Flat feet:* The temptation may be great, but *don't cross your legs.* It may be more comfortable, especially during a long event, but it looks awful. If need be, cross your feet at the ankles; but nothing looks better than having your feet planted firmly on the floor, with your knees close together.
- *Skirting trouble:* Women who have to sit on stage at an event should keep in mind that skirts, especially straight, short ones, tend to ride up when the wearer is seated. On such occasions it's better to *wear pants or longer, fuller skirts*.

Prime Minister Margaret Thatcher, attending the 1990 Economic Summit in Houston, faced a particular, even a peculiar, problem: The Summit's opening event was held outdoors on a broiling Texas summer day. To provide some relief to the world leaders, a machine off to one side blew copious quantities of air conditioning upon them. To keep the Prime Minister's skirt from billowing up around her, Marilyn Monroe-style, small weights were sewn into its hem. Thus "Mrs. T" could keep both a stiff upper lip and a stiff lower hem. (Recalling the ceremony a few years later, Lady Thatcher omitted any reference to the weights but noted that the air conditioning was so powerful that "It was the only time in my political career I went into a meeting with cold feet!")

- **Where to keep your hands:** When standing at official functions, women should copy Queen Elizabeth's practice of **placing one hand atop the other at waist level.** This also creates a handy crook in the arm, perfect for hanging a handbag!

Men should follow President Kennedy's practice of **holding the ring finger of their left hand with the fingers of the right, also at waist level.** It's more attractive than sticking your hands into trouser or coat pockets, and it conveys an air of expectant action.

For both sexes when seated, there are **only three permissible spots to put your hands: Folded in your lap; placed on your knees; or on the arms of the chair.** And just as you should never cross your legs on stage, never cross your arms, either. It looks brusque and impatient.

The Important Person may be (and often is) stopped at any moment by friend and stranger alike to shake hands and talk awhile. Whether or not you're a politician on the prowl for votes, be ready for this by **never carrying anything in your right hand.** Since most people are right-handed, they tend to do exactly this, so you must remember to carry everything in your left hand, leaving the right free for action. This is akin to the earlier rule about never holding a glass in your right hand at a reception.

And while we're on the subject of hands, a delicate matter must be mentioned: When leaving a washroom, **always make certain your hands are completely dry.** Quite frequently, right on the other side of the lavatory door is someone who will want to shake hands with you. When this happens, don't make that poor soul perform the job that a towel should have done ten seconds earlier. (The same rule applies if you have sweaty palms.)

- *Applause!* You may have to applaud, again and again, when a speaker proclaims some platitude about motherhood and country, when an endless list of local officials is introduced, or when all the graduates of a school are announced. But you don't actually have to make the sound of two hands clapping. Simply cup both hands and go through the motion of applauding. It will create a soft, easy-on-the-palms sound like *kwup-kwup*, if that.

Incidentally, have you ever noticed that in giving routine applause, audiences always clap ten times?

AIDE AND COMFORT

If you are a VIP, you may have a bright, young, eager, and (hopefully) able young man or woman assigned as your personal helper. It is a wonderful way for the young person to gain experience and knowledge before becoming an Important Person herself someday.

This job goes by many names. In Washington, it's called a special assistant; in the army, an aide-de-camp; in the navy, a flag lieutenant; in business, an executive assistant; in posh circles in London, a private secretary; and, in unposh ones, a dogsbody.

These helpers plan trips and accompany the boss on them to make sure that everything goes without a hitch—most importantly that the luggage isn't lost. Back in the office, they write speeches, testimony, newspaper columns, and letters. They welcome guests and make sure they are comfortable until the boss can see them. They return telephone calls the boss cannot or does not want to make personally. And at functions, they rescue the boss from angry or adoring conversations that have gone on too long.

In short, having an aide can be both a great help to the VIP and a great learning opportunity for the young person. But, as the VIP, you have certain responsibilities in this almost parental relationship.

For one thing, the aide is not a servant, a slave, a lackey, or (worst of all) a love interest. He or she may make some whopping mistakes, by commission or omission, as young people often do. When these occur, the boss needs to forgive if not forget. Tolerance and forbearance are called for, as well as instruction in how not to mess up next time. After all, what matters in the long run is not the Important Person's precious dignity or ease but the young person's practical education.

*When cameras are lurking about...*Plastic surgery, cosmetics, and hair dye aside, we can't change our looks, and the camera has the diabolical knack of seeing through our best disguises. However, there are some basic defenses to deploy whenever someone pops up with a camera:

- *How to smile:* This would seem natural enough: You just curl up the ends of your mouth and show the pearlies. Well, not quite. The trouble with natural smiling is that it requires working a lot of facial muscles, sometimes with ghastly effects—lines, creases, lopsided lips, and worse. Some people actually look as if they are in severe pain when smiling.

The simple technique, pioneered by the first President Bush, is this: *Just open your mouth and twinkle your eyes.* This involves few facial muscles, displays your dental work, and on film looks like a smile, maybe even better than your "natural" one.

- *Hide your drink!* Even if it's only ginger ale in your glass, you might look like a lush in the town newspaper if a photograph catches you holding a drink. If you can't put down the glass, then hide it behind the back of the person standing next to you.
- *Hitting the bottle:* The plastic bottle of water is a common sight nowadays, often provided without a glass to speakers or panelists. But it looks absolutely awful to hoist the bottle to your lips and take a swig—as Senator Marco Rubio of Florida learned when he paused to wet his whistle while making the Republican response to President Obama's

State of the Union Address in 2013. Unflattering pictures of Rubio and his bottle flew around the Internet and other social media. So, either ask for a glass or try to make it through your appearance without water.

- *Remove that nametag!* This is the aforementioned Third Law of Nametags. Unless the photographer remembers to tell you this and you forget, the nametag will look like a price tag in the photo—not a flattering image, particularly in political gatherings.
- *Take off your sunglasses!* Even the coolest of fashion shades may make you look more like a mafioso or a Latin American dictator than a movie star.
- *Button up!* Men should button their jackets for a photograph and for that matter anytime when on their feet. This tames an errant necktie and hides a paunch.
- *Best foot forward*: In a group shot, people should not line up shoulder-to-shoulder but should **stand sideways, with one foot slightly extended.** This is known as "the Lynn Wyatt pose" in honor of the glamorous international social leader. (The fact there is no bad picture of Mrs. Wyatt shows that people who are frequently photographed instinctively know what does and doesn't look good to a camera.)
- *Don't touch your face in any way if you can help it.* This includes mopping your brow, wiping away tears, blowing your nose, or scratching a body part. All of these can look terrible on film. The best way to look is composed, with a slight smile on your face, except when circumstances demand a sadder look.

Tips for VIPs # 7

DEFENSE AGAINST
THE TRICKY CLICKSTER

VIPs are especially vulnerable to being photographed in unguarded moments. This happens when their mouths are open (eating or talking), when they're yawning, or (worse) when their eyelids are drooping. These occasions may be practically unavoidable, especially at a banquet that's running late.

The most you can do in photographic self-defense is simply to be aware of this risk and be watchful for the raised camera. When cameras are around, don't make a motion or a facial expression without first imagining how it will look on the 10 o'clock news or on the front page of the next day's paper.

*An audience fascinated by buzz words, jargon,
abbreviations, and PowerPoint.*

Chapter 5

"BEFORE I SPEAK, I'D LIKE TO SAY SOMETHING..."

Important Persons are often asked "to say a few words." Many people—researchers say most of us—are terrified of having to stand before a group, small or large, and speak. For some, this fear outranks high bridges, snakes, spiders, and even death!

There are carloads of books on how to make an effective speech, tell a joke, remember the name of the group you're addressing, and so forth. This chapter doesn't aim to replace or restate any of their wisdom.

But whatever you may have to do in the way of public speaking—a committee report, a commencement address, a topical talk, a tribute to someone who's retiring from the company after thirty-five years—there are a few very simple rules, typically observed in the breach.

- The first is: ***Always say something meaningful.*** This doesn't mean announcing a Nobel Prize-winning discovery every time you rise to speak. It doesn't even mean saying something deep. It simply means telling your audience something they may not have known, may never have considered, or may never have heard quite the same way as you express it.

- The second is: ***Always be brief.*** It is absolutely true that no one ever complained about a speech that was too short. Lincoln's talk at Gettysburg had an impact on his audience and on all those who have heard or read it since, not just because of its eloquence but also because of its brevity.

The main speaker that day, incidentally, was not the President but famed orator Edward Everett, who spoke at great length. Impressed by what we now know as the Gettysburg Address, Everett wrote Lincoln, "I could flatter myself [if] I came as near to the central idea of the occasion in two hours as you did in two minutes." Lincoln's reply was equally gracious but didn't dispute the point: "You could not have [made] a short address nor I a long one."[7]

- The third is: ***Speak in simple terms.*** This does not mean speaking down to people. Just the opposite: Those who deploy jargon, buzz phrases, abbreviations, and "big words" can confuse, lose, and even offend an audience, while the speaker who talks in a direct, down-to-earth manner can have a lasting, positive, and even powerful impact.

Think of Patrick Henry: "I know not what course others may take, but as for me, give me liberty or give me death!" Or Lincoln: "That we here highly resolve that these dead shall not have died in vain; that this nation, under God, shall have

---

[7] "Paper Trail", by Nicholas A. Basbanes, *Humanities*, January / February 2014.

a new birth of freedom…" Or FDR: "The only thing we have to fear is fear itself." Or Churchill: "This was their finest hour!" Or Kennedy: "Ask not what your country can do for you; ask what you can do for your country!"

Churchill, perhaps the finest craftsman in English of modern times, once wrote: "Short words are best, and old words when short are best of all." Nothing better illustrates his point than his sentence: All the words are of one syllable, and yet the effect is strong, clear, and elegant.

- The fourth prime point of effective speechmaking is this: **Be pleasant and conversational.** If you can be humorous and the occasion is right, be that, too. But know that one person's humor can be another person's insult. And while humor can be good, jokes can be a problem, especially if the audience has already heard yours (maybe from the previous speaker!). There is also such a thing as a joke that is *too* funny: A story that the audience really likes may be replayed in their minds, over and over, making them miss the serious point you have moved on to make.
- Finally: **Talk about them, not yourself.** You may open with a self-deprecatory reference or joke, but quickly leave the fascinating topic of *you* to praise the organization, the graduates, the day, or the deceased. (Yes, many a eulogist at a funeral talks more about himself than the dear departed.)

There are some other things to remember when you are called on to give a talk:

- **Speak up!** The most basic thing is to make sure the audience can hear you. Don't worry about talking too loudly; the much more common problem is speaking too softly. As soon as you step up to a microphone, adjust it so that it is close to your lips, about the distance of the width of your hand. As you speak, turning your head left and right to look at your entire audience, always keep your lips that close to the microphone.
- **Eyes on the guys:** It's always best to speak without a text. (Notes are fine.) This allows you to make direct eye contact with your audience. But some public utterances are so sensitive, so important, or so unfamiliar that you have to read them. There are a couple of tricks the pros use when they need to read.

One is to **read over the text several times until you are familiar with it.** Then you can frequently raise your eyes from the page and make eye contact, confident that when you need to glance back at the page you'll know exactly where you left off.

The other trick is to **train your eyes to read ahead of the words you're speaking.** Learn to run your fingers along the lines of text just a few words ahead of what you're saying aloud. Through this technique, you'll be simply repeating the words you just read silently. This not only cuts down on verbal stumbles; it allows you to look out at the audience more often.

- **Death by PowerPoint:** Contrary to what many people think, computer aids like PowerPoint tend to work *against* effective public speaking. This is because too many presenters use too many slides, moved for some reason to put their entire talk on the screen. This means slide after gray slide of boring text. Even worse, they often read every word on every slide. This may be greatly appreciated by any illiterates who happen to be in the room, but it's an agony for everyone else. At the very least, such visual aids make the audience look at the screen and not at you.

Far more impactful is to have the audience look only at you and concentrate on what you are saying until you spring on them a few—and only a few—particularly powerful graphs, photos, or words that hammer home the key point(s) you want to make.

Therefore, *use graphics sparingly.* What the great architect Mies van der Rohe said of buildings also applies to speechmaking: *"Less is more."*

- *S-s-stage f-f-fright!* It happens to everyone, even to those who earn their living by speaking in public, namely politicians and actors. The cleverest device to overcome stage fright is one that the great British actor Richard Burton once confided to a television audience. Burton confessed to times when he was seized by stage fright. Surprised, the TV interviewer asked Burton how he dealt with the problem. Sir Richard replied with a smile, *"I clench my toes."*

Even if you're wearing sandals, no one is likely to notice your feet. Way down there you can expel great amounts of nervous energy, while high above your toes you remain calm, serene, and unclenched.

- **The biggest, uh, error of all is, you know, saying "uh" and "you know."** Even news reporters and high officials— and for that matter, the rest of us—pepper and salt our words with "uh" or "ah." And many people throw in "you know" when in truth they (let alone you) *don't* know. Maybe they dread "dead air" and feel they have to have to fill every moment with some sort of sound, even if meaningless.

Broadcasters, politicians, academicians, and bureaucrats think they sound uh-mazingly smart when they pause and ponder before delivering their next set of brilliant words to us: "What the Iranians have been for centuries is, uh, bargainers in the bazaar of, uh, regional affairs! "

But the truly smart thing is to *use* those moments of silence to your advantage. Carefully choose your words and then say them. Not only does this eliminate irritating and senseless noises from your speech, it will actually make people listen more closely to what you're saying.

This parallels the wisdom revealed by a British member of Parliament after he heard a talk by a US senator. "That man is the most brilliant speaker I've heard in America!" the MP exclaimed, to the astonishment of his American host, who thought the senator's remarks completely vapid.

Asked to explain himself, the Brit said slyly, "He knows the secret: *When you have absolutely nothing to say,* **speak slowly!**"

True enough, if-you-talk-very-slowly, your-audience-will-be-waiting-for-every-word!

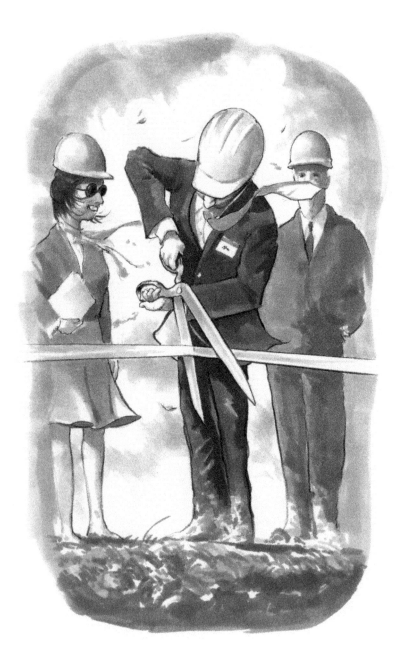

Snip Slip: Look at the camera, not the ribbon.

- Chapter 6 -

CEREMONIES & SOLEMNITIES

You don't have to be a VIP to attend any number of special occasions. Most of them are pleasant and even fun, like graduations, but some can be sad, such as funerals. The Important Person may be more on view than ever at times like these. Many people in the audience may be nervous, uncomfortable, or distraught. But they expect the Important Person to know exactly what to do.

From the planners of the event, who may be rather uncertain or emotionally over-wrought themselves, you may get no help. So at such times the guiding rule should be: Take things slowly. This has the practical effect of giving you time to figure things out, but it also makes you appear dignified, knowledgeable, and orderly—even if in fact you're as lost as everyone else.

Here are some practical rules:

- *Relax: If it isn't your event to run, don't make it one.* Whatever may happen that offends your sense of order or propriety, your job is to do what you've been asked to do—like give the speech—and nothing more.

It's not up to you to stage-whisper guidance to the master of ceremonies, like, "She comes later in the program!" or "He isn't here!" Just do what the MC directs everyone to do, and if this proves to be awkward (such as being asked to sit down after a prayer and then stand up again to give the Pledge of Allegiance to the flag), just smile along with the audience and do it.

After you've been to enough events, you can appreciate the human comedy that's always at its richest when people have to say or do something on stage. Better to just "go with the flow" and enjoy the show, for which you have the best possible seat.

- **Ten-Hut!** A major cause of awkwardness in public comes when flags are presented. If you're a former Marine or Scout, you know what to do, but many others do not.

As soon as the flags are brought forward, stand and remain standing until everyone is asked to be seated. You don't have to be ramrod-straight like a West Point cadet, but simply and comfortably rise to your full height and place your arms at your side.

Only military personnel in uniform, with their headgear on, give the traditional salute. For civilians, the proper thing to do is place your right hand over your heart. *Civilians never give a hand salute.* Yes, presidents often deliver snappy salutes to the Marines stationed at the steps of their helicopters. But they're the commander-in-chief, and no one in the Armed Forces is going to tell them to knock it off. A civilian receiving a military salute should merely acknowledge it with a nod or a word of greeting.

You should give the hand-on-heart salute whenever the national flag passes by and when the first note of the National Anthem is sounded. As the last note ends, count one second and drop the hand salute. (You can also watch and copy the honor guard commander; when he stops saluting, so can you.)

Whenever the national anthem is played, face the flag and render the civilian salute. If there is no flag, simply face the music and place your hand over your heart. You don't have to sing the anthem if your voice isn't up to its demands or if a trained singer is doing the job.

If foreign flags are presented and foreign anthems played, you should follow the same procedure as above. You will not be acting disloyally to your own country or endorsing the other nation's policies by these simple courtesies. After all, any US troops present will all be at attention and saluting.

Tips for VIPs # 9
SNIP, SNAP

If you are ever called upon to open a building or an event in the time-honored fashion, remember the one and only rule: *When cutting a ribbon, look at the camera, not at the ribbon.* Just before the big moment, position the scissors at the right spot, hold the ribbon with your other hand, look out at the spectators, smile, and await the cue to cut. Ready, *snip!* Complete success is guaranteed; you don't have to look down to check.

- *Making remarkably good remarks:* When it comes to giving remarks at a ceremony, the basics of a good speech (covered earlier) also apply: Say something meaningful, be brief, use simple language, speak of the occasion or those being honored rather than yourself, and talk in a pleasant, conversational tone.

Tips for VIPs # 10
SOLEMNLY SWEARING

If you are ever elected or appointed to a public office, you will face the special thrill—and special challenge—of taking an oath, often with family, friends, and associates gathered in your honor. When this occurs, be sure that your right arm forms a right angle and is straight up. Don't look as if you're about to scratch your ear or catch a tennis ball. (This may require some practice in front of a mirror before the big day.)

Continued next page

You may only have to say, "I do" or "So help me God." But if you have to repeat the entire oath, do so in a clear, strong voice. If you muff some words, just smile and plod ahead; it will be just as official. When Barack Obama was sworn in as president in 2009, Chief Justice John Roberts scrambled the words of the oath and went to the White House the next day to administer it correctly—in private. But no one doubted that Obama was legally and officially the president since noon the previous day.

If you're called on to administer an oath, you need to do a little homework ahead of time. No matter how many times you've given the same oath, have it written down on a card to keep in your left hand just in case you suddenly forget the words. And by all means break up the oath into easy, bite-sized phrases for both you and the honoree to say without stumbling. (The dreaded tongue-twister in the federal oath is, "I take this obligation freely, without any mental reservation or purpose of evasion.")

Incidentally, the typical oath-taking ceremony is just that: A dramatic photo-opportunity that often takes place days after the official has signed a document putting her on the government payroll—the oath that really counts. A prominent federal judge refused to participate in oath-taking ceremonies, calling the whole charade "one for the money and two for the show!"

- **Religious services:** The Important Person often has to attend the services of another faith, most commonly weddings and funerals. This may lead to awkward moments: Do I stand or kneel? What are they singing? What do I put in the collection plate?

Once again, *the best way to act is relaxed, composed, and respectful.* The regular attendees will of course know you are a stranger. They will excuse your confusion over the rites of worship (which can vary from church to church even within the same religion) and will offer help.

No one expects you to declare anything or perform something that is against your own religion, but in general, *do what everyone else is doing.* If they're kneeling, you kneel. If they're singing, you sing. If they are reciting, you recite.

As for the collection, give what you would in your own church. Give cash, unless you want credit for the contribution and might therefore leave a check with your name and address on it. In any case, *have your donation ready* so you don't have to fumble around when the plate or collection bag comes to you. Also, be advised that some churches have multiple collections, especially when there a number of special guests present!

- *Consolations:* It may fall your sad duty to attend a funeral or memorial service, perhaps one for several people, such as for soldiers or firefighters killed in the line of duty. You may have to give a memorial address or eulogy. In this talk, employ brevity, genuine sentiment, tribute, quotation, and if possible personal reminiscence in the hope of doing an adequate job of praising the one(s) you're there to mourn. Once again, don't talk about yourself, unless you're a minor figure in a story about the deceased.

Then will come the hardest thing of all: Greeting the family. There are no words to make sobbing survivors feel instantly better. If you knew the deceased, you can credibly say something like, "He was a wonderful man" or "I was proud to know your mother." If you didn't, you should avoid spouting such lofty platitudes as, "He has gone to a much better place!" or "I'm sure all will be well." As inadequate and obvious as it sounds, a simple "I'm sorry" is about the best you can say.

If you are a VIP, your mere presence says something, in which case you need only shake or clasp hands with each family member and give whatever soft words of greeting come naturally. There may be welcome breaks at even these most doleful of occasions, as when you come to a baby or other small child, sparking a smile and a cheerful exchange with the parent.

- *Crying in Public:* With tears, as with beads of sweat, it's better just to *let them flow* than to dab them with a handkerchief. This is especially true if you're embarrassed by tears, for the unwiped tear is harder for a camera or an audience to see. (Makeup can always be repaired later.) Even if you're not embarrassed by weeping, you will look more stoic and composed by not hauling out the hanky.
- *Embracing:* Whatever else Bill Clinton may have done for America, he made it wholly acceptable for men to hug in public. The body count by both his successors has been equally high. Of course, the Latino *abrazo* and its equivalents in Middle Eastern and Eastern European cultures are becoming more common as America's

population becomes ever richer with immigrants. Even men from precincts where croquet still reigns can now go through these rituals without hesitating, stiffening, or blushing. (This has never been a problem with women, who are natural huggers.)

Men may now also hug and kiss women in public (as when arriving on stage for an event) without—necessarily—incurring a lurid reputation. Maybe we have Bill to thank for this, too.

In short, *do whatever comes naturally.* Except in certain ethnic neighborhoods, hugging is still only optional, not required. And if you are hugged, act as if you're enjoying it. This is what Queen Elizabeth did on a visit to Washington in 1991. A community leader with an effusive personality suddenly embraced Her Majesty, as she did everyone else. Though this shattered centuries of royal protocol, the Queen, a good trooper, maintained a smile throughout the brief ordeal.

Tips for VIPs # 11
HANDING IT OVER

When receiving a diploma, certificate, or award, many people act like octopuses—unsure which arm to use for the simple one-two act of shaking hands and collecting the prize object. In their confusion, they may even drop it.

Here is how to prevent lifelong embarrassment for the graduate and make all turn out well for Granny taking the snap.

As the proud but nervous recipient starts across the stage, hold the diploma or award in your left hand alongside your leg, temporarily out of sight from the eager recipient. Instead of looking at the diploma, she will see you, standing there with a big smile and an outstretched right hand. This tends to put the graduate at ease and simplifies matters, since everyone knows how to shake hands.

Once your right hands are joined, you can then produce the diploma or award with your left. This not only eliminates the recipient's confusion, it makes for a much better picture.

As you do this, say whatever pat phrase you've chosen for the occasion, like "Congratulations!" or "Well done!" or "Good luck!" (It won't matter what you say to the recipient, for whom the whole thing is a big buzz.)

Finally, as the handshake ends, drop your right hand in a natural way alongside your leg. This will unobtrusively wipe away the souvenir of the sweaty palm you've just encountered!

"I'm really glad you asked that question...Uh, let me say, Genevieve...I mean..."

Chapter 7

MESS WITH THE PRESS
WITH LESS DISTRESS

From a CEO besieged by reporters outside a courthouse to the local club president eager to publicize a forthcoming event, few Important People can escape the press.

Biased, nosy, insulting, aggressive, and slovenly *or* fair, polite, deferential, and well-groomed, reporters have one thing in common: They're just trying to get the story. Dealing with the press is an essential part of any Important Person's job—the more so the higher up you go.

While meeting the press has to be endured, it doesn't have to be a harrowing experience. It may not be especially *fun*, but there are several proven techniques for dealing with—and surviving—the experience. It's even possible to make valuable allies, if not close friends, in the process.

- The first thing to remember is that **the press always has the last word.** This truth was captured by whoever first warned, "Never argue with someone who buys ink by the barrel." You can state your side of an issue to a reporter as forcefully as you want, but in the end the reporter will have newsprint and air time at her disposal and you won't.

"Wooing the press is an exercise roughly akin to picnicking with a tiger," observed Maureen Dowd of *The New York Times*, herself a feared feline. "You might enjoy the meal, but the tiger always eats last."

- A frequent criticism of the press is that it's biased, usually against conservatives or Republicans or big business. True, most journalists are left-of-center in their politics, but the real slogan of the working press is not "Comes the revolution!" but *"Down with those who are up, and up with those who are down!"* Many reporters will say they "comfort the afflicted and afflict the comfortable." And since those who are "up" tend to be rich and powerful people, many of whom are conservative or Republican, this distinction may be of small relief to those who find themselves a target of the press. The thing reporters most like is "a good story," and all good stories need heroes and villains.

The late David Broder of *The Washington Post*, who was dean of American political reporters, observed that, "Reporters are essentially storytellers, heirs to a narrative tradition as old as mankind. Stories have settings and characters and plot lines. Whether we [reporters] acknowledge it or not, we are constantly devising the scripts we think appropriate for the events we are covering."[8]

---

[8] David S. Broder. *Behind the Front Page.* New York: Simon & Schuster, 1987

Tony Hayward, CEO of BP at the time of the great Gulf of Mexico oil spill of 2010, erred fatally when he groused to the press, "I'd like to get my life back." Whatever else Hayward may have said about the spill, these few words made him seem cold and self-absorbed. He thus became the perfect foil for reporters of the "down with those who are up" school, eager to write that BP was unconcerned with the lives of shrimpers and cormorants alike.

So, in dealing with the press, the Important Person should always try—*try*—to guide the story in the most positive way possible. The CEO under scrutiny will want to say things that show him or her to be reasonable, fair, innovative, empathetic, and at the very least innocent. At the other end of the scale, the club president will want to make the coming bake sale seem fun and interesting.

- Dan Rather, the longtime reporter and news anchor for CBS, has a useful axiom for those who have to deal with the press: ***There are only three ways to answer a reporter's question:***

  1. ***I know and I'll tell you.***
  2. ***I know and I can't tell you. (Here's why…)***
  3. ***I don't know.***

Strict adherence to this simple code may not make you a reporter's favorite news source. But you may earn credit for candor, and that might give you the benefit of the doubt next time.

- It's important to **know the rules of talking to the press** and to make sure that you and the reporter agree on these *before* the interview.

On the record means that anything you say may be used by the reporter and that you can be quoted by name.

Off the record means that a casual conversation or remark cannot be quoted.

On background means that you can be quoted but described only in some general way, like a "high government official," "White House aide," or "knowledgeable source." (Henry Kissinger allowed himself to be quoted as "an official traveling on the Secretary of State's plane.")

On deep background means that the information is provided for the reporter's general understanding and cannot be quoted in any form.

Regardless how this book defines the above terms, you need to know how the *reporter* defines them before you start talking. After the interview you can't suddenly say, "Oh, that was all off the record!" Unless the reporter is a good friend or sees value in continuing a relationship with you, he or she may close their notebook with a smile and say, "Sorry; too late!"

Reporters always want to use real names and will often try to wheedle the news source into going on the record. Some may betray both confidences and sources. When this happens, the victim has few options. (See the above item about people who buy barrels of ink.)

- Whatever you do, ***don't think you can make the press go away by ignoring them***. You might succeed once or twice, but your attitude will only convince them that you have something to hide—and that the story is even juicier than they imagined.

Asked by the Navy staff what their press policy should be during World War II, the frosty chief of naval operations, Admiral Ernest O. King, replied: "Don't tell them anything, except that when it's over, tell them who won."

- When asked a tough question, those best at handling the press have a knack for **figuring out what to say before speaking a word**. In an instant, their mental computers take the words they are ready to say and imagine them in a newspaper headline or a radio-TV sound bite. If they don't like the way these might look or sound, they think of something else and run *that* statement through their noggins. Only when satisfied with an answer do they start talking. The pros can run this mental analysis in just one or two seconds. This is what they're doing while saying, "Sam, I'm really glad you asked that question!"
- What if asked a tough question that you don't want to answer at all? Replying "no comment" may make you appear shifty. So, when ordinarily golden-tongued politicians and business leaders are hit with such questions, they **suddenly become grossly inarticulate**—starting and stopping sentences, never quite completing a discreet thought, and in general uttering complete mush.

The result is something that won't be quoted because it makes no sense. ("What we have to do…Uh, let me say, Genevieve, that…You have to remember…I mean…") The dogged reporter can continue to ask questions, but, faced with more mush, she may ultimately give up in disgust. The news source is left smiling sweetly: After all, he *did* respond to the question!

A variation on this tactic is to **say what you want to see in print or hear over the air, even if it has nothing to do with the question you are asked.** Reporters don't like this and may keep hurling their original question at you, and you may not be quoted at all. But that may be just fine with you.

A final bit of press wisdom was given by the late Maxine Messinger, a Houston gossip columnist who recycled her tidbits in the morning paper for drive-time radio listeners. Maxine would close every report with a warning: **"Remember: If you don't want to hear about it on the radio, don't do it!"**

Never forget that parking police are really important!

- Chapter 8 -

THE OFFICIAL VISIT

This particular challenge can range from a simple visit to a daycare center by a delegation of Junior Leaguers to the inspection of a troubled hospital by a high-ranking government official, complete with aides, reporters, cameras, and onlookers. In both circumstance, the hosts will be very anxious to please, especially if money and job futures are at stake.

The key thing to remember throughout the visit is that **your hosts may be extremely nervous**. In some cases, they may have good reason, fearing that you may uncover evidence of their boobery or deceit. In most cases, though, they are simply worried that you may leave with a poor impression.

Your job is just to see what there is to be seen (and on occasion dig out the truth). And **the best way to come across is pleasant, serene, interested, and alert**—even if you're not any of these.

Here is how to accomplish the purpose of your visit while putting people at ease and making them feel appreciated.

- First of all, **be on time!** King Edward VII, the son of Queen Victoria, once said, "Promptness is the courtesy of princes." He even ordered all the clocks in his palaces set half an hour ahead so he would never keep anyone waiting. (He told his son, the future King George V: "It is very hard work being a prince. You must think all the time that other people matter more than yourself.")
- *The Arrival:* A VIP arrives in a car driven by someone else, which eliminates any worries about parking. It also means you can immediately smile at the eager faces of the people waiting to greet you. If you're just a run-of-the-mill Important Person who has to drive your own car, you'll be fortunate if your hosts remembered to set aside a place for you to park. Remember that even though you're an Important Person, parking police are *really* important, and you can be ticketed and towed like all mortals.

Tips for VIPs # 12
GETTING OUT OF THE CAR

Whether you're riding in the back or in the front seat, as soon as the door is opened swing both your legs out of the car. This will allow you to stand up immediately and shake hands with the person or group of people waiting to greet you. It also makes for a better picture.

- *The folks in the background*: Your escort probably will be the Big Boss and his or her top assistants, who will stick closely to you throughout the visit. But on the sidewalk, at the entrance, lining a hallway, or in a room may be others (and maybe many others) in the organization you're visiting. They may be the people who truly make the place work: the nurses, teachers, factory hands, sailors, etc. As soon as you see them, walk over to say hello and thank them for their hospitality or for doing their job. Your hosts may fret that this will put you behind schedule, but it is powerfully effective with the people who count the most.

If you can't shake hands with each person, you should *make eye contact with everyone, smile, and say a simple hello or word of thanks*.

Tips for VIPs # 13
MY PEOPLE, MY PEOPLE

If people waiting to see you are lined up on both sides of the corridor or lane through which you're walking, copy the practice of Queen Elizabeth II: She smiles at people she passes on one side and then, still walking forward, turns her head and shoulders to smile back at the people she passed on the other side. A few paces onward, she turns again, sweeping backward to front, and repeats the process. To the maximum extent possible, she establishes eye contact with everyone, who can excitedly claim, "She smiled at me!"

You may not have quite the same effect, but you'll acknowledge everyone and show that you appreciate the hospitality and efforts.

- *Beware the ups and downs:* President Gerald Ford was a fine man, a college athlete, and a hard-working chief executive in difficult times. And yet he was portrayed to Americans in the mid-1970s as a clumsy oaf, due to some well-photographed stumbles on stairs. Since the days of John F. Kennedy, American presidents and other politicians have been expected to display "vigor" (which JFK pronounced "vigah"), always moving swiftly, with no points given for caution. Even so, *when going up or down stairs, run your hand along the handrail,* ready to grasp it tightly in case you miss a step. When going in either direction, but especially heading downstairs, *arch your back* so that if you do stumble, you won't fall face-forward.

- *Taking the tour:* The Important Person will often be asked to "tour the premises." On these walkarounds, which may be totally baffling or boring, you must *always appear interested in what you're seeing*. Your only permissible reactions lie in the zone ranging from curiosity to fascination. Sometimes you may not be able to hear your escort over the noise of an assembly line or an engine room. But this doesn't allow you to appear bored or distracted. While looking straight at the inaudible lecturer or at the machine, you can let your mind wander to whatever else suits your fancy, interjecting a question now and then to indicate your interest.

(It must be admitted that the first President Bush got slammed hard politically when he observed this rule. He was touring a trade show, at which his host demonstrated how quickly bar-coded merchandise can be rung up in supermarkets. Bush expressed interest in this technology, familiar to all American grocery shoppers, after which he was attacked for being "out of touch" with the lives of ordinary people.)

- *Finding out the truth:* This is always tricky, especially if you don't have subpoena power. There are two ways of learning what's really going on—or, better put, to have the slightest hope of learning it if your hosts have something to hide.

1. The first method is to *ask the right questions*. Your hosts may not exactly lie to you, but they may give you only a partial truth. They do this when a completely honest answer might embarrass them or cause problems, like extra work.

In one of Peter Sellers's *Pink Panther* movies, the hapless Inspector Clouseau asks a hotel clerk, "Does your dog bite?" The clerk says no, whereupon Clouseau bends down to pet a nearby dog. When the cur chomps down on the inspector's hand, Clouseau hotly addresses the clerk, "You said your dog does not bite!" The clerk shrugs and says, "That is not my dog."

So, remember: You often need to *keep asking questions from all different angles* to get the full story.

The basic crowbar line of questioning is about change: What has changed? What do they want to change? What's kept change from happening? This tends to work because your hosts may have an interest in keeping things as they are— or, if they want change, they want it on their terms and at their pace.

2. The second means of getting at the truth on an official visit is to **encourage people, directly or subtly, sooner or later, to come forward**, and tell it to you.

This may be the practical result of your meeting the worker bees during your visit. A smile or warm greeting may just embolden someone to tell you what the bosses don't want you to know. This person may boldly approach you during a meal or reception, or he may quietly inform you "what's really going on around here" by mail or message after you leave. Yes, he may be a hothead, but within every hothead may burn the fire of truth, ready to blow the place apart.

- When you get back to your home or office, **write notes of thanks**, the more the better. Just like a smile or a warm word, a simple thank-you note from an Important Person is something the recipient will appreciate and possibly keep forever.

The first George Bush climbed to the White House on the stack of personal notes he had written over his lifetime. Bush got into this admirable habit because his mother made him write thank-you notes as soon as he had returned from someone's house. Good manners became in time an immensely successful political tool.

It's a tool that anyone can use. As effective as personal notes are, very few people write them these days. Their rarity only magnifies the impact on the recipient. We live today in a world of portable telephones, electronic mail, web postings, and text messages in which person-to-person contacts by the billions are conducted soullessly every hour. In such an environment, the person who invests the brief amount of time required to take paper and pen and express thanks or sympathy is a stand-out.

Something else the senior President Bush proved with his famous blue-bordered notes is that just *a few lines written by hand mean far more than a much longer formal letter or email.* The intimate nature of such notes is a wonderful way to convey friendship, defuse anger, or respond to a request for a favor.

Someone hoping to be ambassador to a tropic paradise might have gotten a note scrawled by Bush on presidential stationery saying, "Great to hear from you. We'll see what we can do." In the end, the person may never have gotten an embassy, but he couldn't be *too* mad. After all, he had a note that the president of the United States wrote him personally.

So, the lesson is short and simple: Personal notes win votes!

"The real heroes are the people who make committees work."

Chapter 9

THE IMPORTANT PERSON IN CHARGE

Your status as an Important Person could date from the moment your boss asks you to chair a committee. This may be the first test of leadership in your life, and much may ride on how well you do: Your boss may be watching to see if you can handle responsibility. A worthy project may or may not get the money it needs. A nettlesome problem for your business or community may or may not be solved. Or the practice schedule for a kids' soccer team may need to be drawn up.

No matter how small or brief or non-historic the committee, you are now in charge. And when you are, there are some things to keep in mind:

- *A chair is not a piece of furniture:* This is a time that needs leadership more than ever, and yet since the 1960s there has been a horror of "elitism" and hierarchies. The word "chairman" was replaced by "chair," which symbolized the passing of leadership skills from humans to pieces of wood.

This horizontal model of organization may work for a poetry club but not for most anything else. No group that aims to accomplish its goal can be run for long on a nicey-nice "consensus." Eventually, fraternity and sorority collapse into frustration. A leaderless band of brothers (or sisters, or both) may manage to share their thoughts, listen to different ideas, speak with careful concern for each other's sensitivities, and eventually maunder on to a conclusion. But this can consume a lot of time, wasted in the name of not making anyone feel bad. It should be no surprise that the results from such tortured and lengthy sessions are often mushy or mangled. As a wit once observed, a camel is a horse designed by a committee.

The first thing to recognize is that **someone has to be in charge, and right now it's you.** It is not "elitist" to have a leader or to be a leader, and tender feelings need not be hurt along the road to a real decision. All depends on the skills of the person in (but not morphed into) the chair.

- *Tempus fidgets:* Perhaps the most effective thing a presiding officer can do is to **declare right at the start that the meeting will end in a fair but finite amount of time**, for instance one hour. This will force members to pay attention to the business at hand and not lose valuable time talking about last night's ball game. No one likes long meetings, anyway.

This gambit also provides the leader with a handy, non-lethal club to hold over the group, reminding them that they need to keep moving toward a conclusion. If, at the end of the declared length of time, the group hasn't quite reached a decision, the leader can stretch the schedule a little bit to get them there.

- *My way or the "aye" way:* A good leader should have at least a general idea of what she wants to accomplish. This doesn't mean the leader has to be a dictator; but, since people often need some direction, the presiding officer should *have some sort of plan in mind*. When possible, she can nudge the group in that direction. Or, more cleverly, she can enlist an ally in the group to propose and advocate that point of view, allowing her to applaud such a splendid suggestion.
- *Discussion without concussion:* Within the agreed time limit, the leader should *let everyone speak*, encouraging the quieter or more timid members to have their say, too. There is no reason why vigorous debate has to be personally wounding. It tests the sense and worthiness of all ideas. This is one of the reasons why democracy is the best form of government, despite its frequent messiness.

The leader should ask questions to sharpen the group's focus on what's being discussed and to keep members from tiresomely going over the same points. And as the group reaches a conclusion, he should have them examine it from different perspectives to make sure that the proposed solution is the right one and that all flaws have been discovered.

The result should be a clear, concrete statement or plan of action—not some murky "consensus." Prime Minister Thatcher once observed: "A consensus seems to be the process of abandoning all belief in search of something in which no one believes but to which no one objects."

- *Is that what we did?* As soon as possible after the meeting, the leader should *send a memo to all participants summing up what was discussed and what was decided.* This allows members with different impressions of what happened to raise their protest and either get the record corrected or concur with the leader's recollection.
- Finally, the leader should *tell higher authority what the meeting decided and be an advocate for its recommendation.* The report should acknowledge all views, including those contrary to the majority's opinion. This will give those on top a full picture of the situation, and you will gain the gratitude and respect of the minority, even if they are in disagreement.

It is a tricky business to lead a group to a conclusion while allowing all opinions to be aired. This is why it is not "elitist" to give full and clear responsibility to whoever has to chair a committee or board. It is also why Bill Moyers, a former top aide to President Lyndon Johnson, once said, "The real heroes are the people who make committees work."

"No, thanks. I had one of these as a pet when I was a kid."

Chapter 10

IMPORTANTS ABROAD

VIPs frequently get on executive aircraft and travel to distant shores. The limousines, massed troops, anthems, and deep *salaams* that await them are what mark them as truly important. (PS: They all love it!)

Sometimes it is the mere act of going abroad on business that converts an ordinary company employee into an Important Person, because to your foreign hosts you *are* the company. This may hit you with a double challenge: Accomplishing the business of your trip while acting the way your hosts expect of an important visitor.

There are shelves of books that tell you about bowing in Japan, about eating with the right hand in Arab countries, about late dinners in Latin America, and so forth. But here are some pointers that work worldwide:

- *May I present my card?* Other cultures place greater emphasis on rank and title than do Americans. Therefore, *pack along a plentiful supply of business cards*. What is plentiful?" Estimate the most cards you think you'll need—and then *double* that number.

The Asian etiquette when exchanging business cards should apply anywhere on the globe: Upon receiving someone's card, take a moment to read it, nodding in honor and appreciation of the other person's position.

- *May I present my present?* A business practice observed more often overseas than in the United States is gift-giving. Before leaving on your trip, *find out the key people you will meet and what would be an appropriate gift for them.*

In general, people overseas are interested in where you live, so a good gift is a high-quality book of pictures about your city or state, or about some special aspect of life there (cowboys, lobstermen, tribal crafts). For the miscellaneous people who will be helping you—like guides, drivers, and interpreters—bring plenty of small gifts—like key rings, pens, or pins with your national or state flag— that you can easily carry in your pocket or purse.

These gifts may require you to take an extra bag—which is just as well, for you may need it to bring back all the gifts (usually much nicer) that they will give *you*.

- *Giving shorts short shrift:* Plan to *dress more conservatively and more formally abroad than in the United States*. During weekdays this means dark business suits and dresses, white shirts, and neckties. Some (modest) casual clothes may be appropriate for sightseeing on weekends or on some evenings. But unless you'll be spending time in a resort, leave your shorts at home.

- *Ah yes, Brazil: where the nuts come from!* Before you travel abroad, **study the basic facts about the country you'll be visiting**. This may seem an obvious thing to do, and yet in an era when Americans can travel abroad more easily than pass a simple geography exam, many people remain a bit fuzzy on the difference between Belgium and the Netherlands or between India and Pakistan. A good source of such information is the "Countries and Regions" section of the U.S. State Department website, *www.state.gov*.

- *Howzat?* If your conversation or negotiation is being interpreted, there is a simple etiquette to follow. You may not understand a word of the language the other person is speaking, but you should still pay attention as if you do. To glance around the room or study the papers in front of you while your foreign host is speaking is impolite. **Look at the other person, including when the interpreter is translating.** Every now and then, glance at the interpreter to indicate appreciation for his or her hard work.

What do you do when you're on your own in a non-English-speaking country? Before you leave home, *invest in a small phrasebook* for the language of that country. The best ones are color-coded for fast reference to food, travel, shopping, and emergencies. If you can't quite pronounce the words, simply point to that expression in the book. In a shop or marketplace where no one speaks your language, the calculator feature on your phone will allow both you and the seller to bargain wordlessly.

Wherever you are, however briefly you may be there, and no matter if you have a fulltime translator at your side, it's always courteous, useful, and fun to *learn and use the following words in the local language:*

Hello

Goodbye

Please

Thank you

How much?

Yes

No

- *A lovely land, full of charming animals*: Your hosts will often ask what you think of their country. Sometimes this will be done with as much anxiety as curiosity, for fear you may think their country is backward, dirty, or otherwise disagreeable. When you answer their question, remember to *praise the people first, the scenery and animals afterwards.* ("The people here are so warm and friendly!")

This is an especially good thing to do in countries that indeed are backward, dirty, or otherwise disagreeable. Your hosts will be delighted by your answer.

- *The uncrinkled nose, the uncurled lip, the unwinced eye, the uncritical word:* In the same vein, if you do have some unflattering observations about the country you're visiting, save them until you get home. Your senses may indeed be assaulted by some fairly terrible smells, sights, and sounds. But to the extent you can, *pretend you do not notice*. Your hosts will be watching your every twitch to see if you are upset about being in their country.

- *"This is raw <u>what</u>?"* Coping with unfamiliar food is perhaps the greatest challenge about being abroad, and this doesn't even include an upset tummy. Your hosts, sometimes with pride and great expense, may present you with delicacies you last saw in an aquarium, a cage, or on a garden wall.

You should *taste everything* to show your gratitude to your hosts, your appreciation of local cuisine, and your good sportsmanship. You don't have to eat it all, and you don't have to ask for seconds. (To stave off hunger pangs, *pack along plenty of filling snacks* like peanut butter crackers or granola bars to eat in your hotel room before or after such meals.)

- *Night time may be work time:* In many parts of the world—Latin America, China, and the Middle East, in particular—you should be prepared for meals and meetings at very late hours. So, to seal the deal, *take naps when you can!*

Also, in many societies, nothing is ever done quickly, at least not by impatient American standards. Your prospective customer or client may in fact use time against you, keeping you in your hotel room for hours and even days, waiting for a phone call that finally announces a meeting or a decision. So, *bring plenty of books (or puzzles or knitting) and a whole lot more patience.*

Finally, remember Mark Twain's warning: "The gentle reader will never, never know what a consummate ass he can become until he goes abroad."[9]

---

[9] Mark Twain. *The Innocents Abroad.* The Library of America: New York, 1984

Hey, Big Guy: Don't forget us!

- *Chapter 11* -

SPOUSE & FAMILY

No woman married to an Important Person is ever merely his wife. And as married women have acquired significant positions in government, business, the professions, and community life in general, no husband need lose his own identity. This is as things should be, but old roles and expectations can still create awkward situations.

- *Who is that lady I see you with?* First of all, ***always introduce your spouse and do so by name***, never just, "This is my wife" or "This is my husband."

Likewise, in conversation it is always better to ***refer to your spouse by her or his name***: "Last summer, when Tom and I were driving through Montana…"

- *The Invisible Man (or Woman):* To ensure that your spouse is not forgotten at an official event, ***the Important Person must remember to do the remembering***. You must make frequent introductions of and references to your spouse. You should also invite him or her to answer a question or to make an observation, especially if it's in your spouse's area of specialty.

You also need to keep checking to **make sure she or he is still there with you**. All too often, eager hosts, concentrating totally on you, have ignored your spouse since you both arrived.

Sometimes your hosts will speak directly to the Important Person and never so much as glance at the spouse sitting nearby. (This sort of thing happens quite frequently in male-dominated societies abroad, but also in the United States.) Once again, it is up to the Important Person to **include the spouse in the discussion** by breaking eye contact with the host and looking over at the spouse, by gesturing in his or her direction, and by pulling him or her into the conversation.

- **The spouse as extender:** Franklin Roosevelt used to refer to Eleanor as "my eyes and ears." Given the demands of his job and his physical disability, she was also his legs. She could do what he could not, namely travel frequently and actively throughout the country to see social conditions at first hand.

There is no question that a willing and able spouse can be a powerful second front in a public life. One needn't be an Eleanor Roosevelt (or, in our day, a Hillary Clinton, a Laura Bush, or a Michelle Obama) to perform this highly useful role. The spouse of an Important Person who is, for instance, visiting a hospital or military base can get around and see things that the main party may not see. She or he can ask probing questions that the Important Person did not or would not ask. Just before departure, the spouse can raise issues or problems he or she observed or learned during the visit. This may prove discomforting to the hosts, but while they squirm the Important Person can smile serenely, grateful for the valuable disclosure.

- **The Junior Important People:** The children of moms or dads in highly-visible roles are in a particularly vulnerable situation. Young people deserve (and expect) a lot of attention normally. This becomes all the harder to get when a parent is an Important Person and in a sense belongs to another, larger, public family.

Sometimes literally pushed aside in the hubbub of a public event as people rush up to greet the star of the family, the children of some Important Persons may act up, as if to shout, "Look at *me*!" Others nurse deep and smoldering resentments. (Asked what he did in his father's campaigns, the son of a well-known politician replied, "I'm a smiler.") Some enjoy the spotlight too much, with embarrassing consequences. The rare few, usually older children, take the whole crazy scene with good nature and value the special occasions and opportunities that come with their parent's role.

The clear message for the Important Person with a family is this: *Just as you can't leave young children physically, you can't leave them emotionally, either.* This means making a greater effort to spend time with them outside of official duties. They should be included in public functions (especially the fun ones) so they feel more a part of the team. And ask your host to make arrangements for your kids to pass the time pleasurably while you're doing the "boring stuff."

WHAT HAVE WE SPAWNED?

Either by fascination or obligation, many children of Important Persons have gone into public service on their own. The Adamses, Roosevelts, Kennedys, Rockefellers, and Bushes spawned generations of public servants, but the champions may be the Tafts. When her grade school class had to write a family history, a young Taft produced the following: "My great-great grandfather was attorney general. My great-grandfather was president and chief justice. My grandfather was a United States senator. My father was ambassador to Ireland. I am a Brownie."

- Conclusion -

YOU MUST REMEMBER THIS

This book has sought to instill a sense of how to act if you are, suddenly become, or aim to be an Important Person. This sense is more valuable than all the helpful hints about coping with nametags, introductions, banquets, and the rest. It can be easily summarized:

- Anyone can become an Important Person and assume a leadership role, sometimes suddenly.
- People expect the Important Person to look and act in a way befitting this role.
- An Important Person always acts composed, comfortable, confident, and considerate.
- An Important Person is never snooty, cold, or impolite.
- *An Important Person makes others feel at ease, recognized, and appreciated.*

◆ ◆ ◆

The story is told of the president of the tiny Sandersville Railroad in central Georgia, who one day in the 1890s wrote the president of the mighty Pennsylvania Railroad proposing that they exchange passes on each other's line. The Pennsy president exploded at this impertinence, noting that his railroad had thousands of miles of track in several states while the Sandersville line ran over just three miles of track in one county.

Responding to this blast, the Georgian wrote: "It is true that my railroad may not be as long as yours, but, sir, it is just as wide!"[10]

The lesson of this story is that no matter how important we or another person may be, we are linked by our common humanity. And how Important People act is nothing less than the way we want everyone to treat us.

[10] "A Long, Arduous March Toward Standardization," by Achsah Nesmith, *Smithsonian*, March 1985.

ABOUT THE AUTHOR

Chase Untermeyer has been an Important Person many times and at many levels. Now a businessman, he was a state legislator and port commissioner in Texas; an assistant secretary of the Navy in the Pentagon; a senior aide to the first President Bush; director of the Voice of America; and United States ambassador to Qatar. He and his wife Diana (who met when they were both on the White House staff) live in Houston with their daughter Elly, a student at Stanford University.